100

things you should know about

KNIGHTS & CASTLES

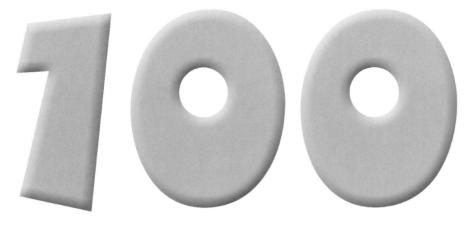

100
things you should know about
KNIGHTS & CASTLES

Jane Walker
Consultant: Richard Tames

Miles Kelly
PUBLISHING

First published in 2001 by
Miles Kelly Publishing Ltd
Bardfield Centre, Great Bardfield, Essex, CM7 4SL

Copyright © Miles Kelly Publishing 2001

4 6 8 10 9 7 5 3

Publishing Director: Anne Marshall
Project Editor: Neil de Cort
Design: Angela Ashton, Joe Jones
Design Manager: Joe Jones
Picture Research: Liberty Newton
Indexing, Proof Reading: Lynn Bresler

ISBN 1-84236-002-7

Printed in China

ACKNOWLEDGEMENTS
The Publishers would like to thank the following artists who have
contributed to this book:

Richard Berridge/ Specs Art   John James/ Temple Rogers
Vanessa Card   Janos Marffy
Nicholas Forder   Angus McBride
Mike Foster/ Maltings   Martin Sanders
Partnership   Nik Spender/ Advocate
Terry Gabbey/ AFA   Roger Stewart
Luigi Galante/ Studio Galante   Rudi Vizi
Sally Holmes   Mike White/ Temple Rogers
Richard Hook/ Linden Artists

Cartoons by Mark Davies at Mackerel

Contents

Castle life

1 **A castle was both a home and a fortress in the Middle Ages.** It provided shelter for a king or a lord and his family, and it allowed him to defend his lands. Castles were also places where soldiers were stationed, wrong doers were imprisoned, courts settled disputes, weapons, and armor were made, and great banquets and tournaments were held.

In the beginning

2 The first castles were mostly built from wood on top of a hill. Sometimes castle builders piled up soil to make the hill artificially. On top of the hill, called a motte, stood a wooden tower, or keep. This was the central part of the castle and the easiest part to defend.

▼ This is a motte and bailey castle. The Normans from France introduced this kind of castle in the 1000s, and it soon became popular across Europe.

◄ Castles and forts have been built all over the world since the earliest times. This is the fortified town of Great Zimbabwe, in modern day Zimbabwe. The oldest part dates from the 700s.

► By the 1500s the Japanese were building strong, permanent castles of their own. Castles were often built with different layers to fire on the enemy from different heights.

3 At the bottom of the motte was a courtyard called a bailey. It was usually surrounded by a wooden fence. Castle builders dug a deep ditch, called a moat, all around the outside of the motte and bailey. They often filled the moat with water. Moats were designed to stop attackers reaching the castle walls.

◄ For extra protection, a wooden fence was often built around the top of the motte. The top of each wooden plank was shaped into a point to make it harder for the enemy to climb over.

I DON'T BELIEVE IT!

The builders of the early wooden castles covered the walls with wet leather—to stop them from burning down.

4 Wooden castles were not very strong—and they caught fire easily. From around 1100 onwards, people began to build castles in stone. A stone castle gave better protection against attack, fire, and cold rainy weather.

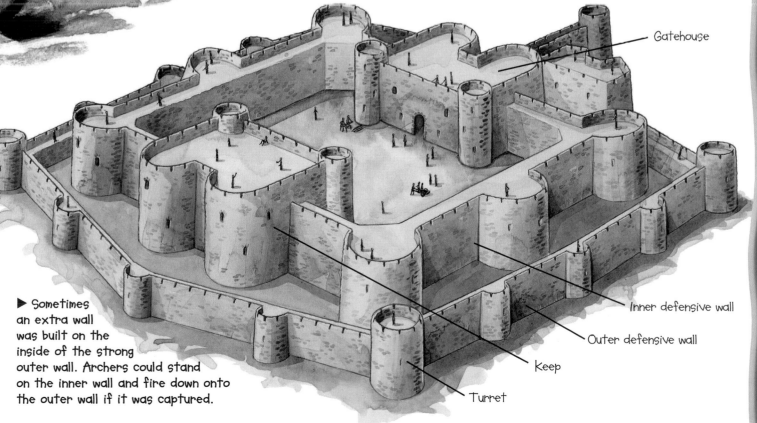

Gatehouse

Inner defensive wall

Outer defensive wall

Keep

Turret

▶ Sometimes an extra wall was built on the inside of the strong outer wall. Archers could stand on the inner wall and fire down onto the outer wall if it was captured.

Building a castle

5 **The best place to build a castle was on top of a hill.** A hilltop position gave good views over the surrounding countryside, and made it harder for an enemy to launch a surprise attack. Sometimes a castle was built on the banks of a river or lake, and its waters were used to create a moat.

6

The lord of the castle and his family lived in the safest part of the castle—the keep.

The walls of the keep were built to be very strong, and at least 12ft (3.7m) thick in some castles. Inside the keep were large rooms for receiving visitors and holding banquets, as well as smaller storerooms and guardrooms. The family's bedrooms were on the top floor of the keep. All these rooms and defenses made building a castle very slow and expensive.

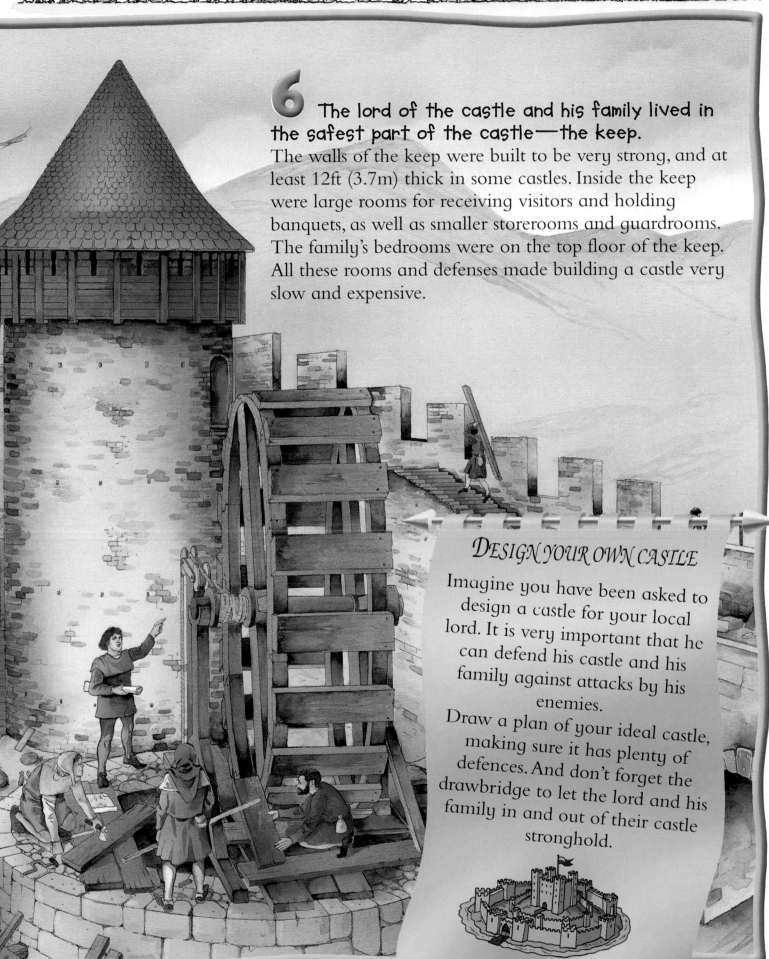

DESIGN YOUR OWN CASTLE

Imagine you have been asked to design a castle for your local lord. It is very important that he can defend his castle and his family against attacks by his enemies.

Draw a plan of your ideal castle, making sure it has plenty of defences. And don't forget the drawbridge to let the lord and his family in and out of their castle stronghold.

Who's who in the castle

7 A castle was the home of an important and powerful person, such as a king, a lord, or a knight. The lord of the castle controlled the castle itself, as well as the lands and people around it. The lady of the castle was in charge of the day-to-day running of the castle. She controlled the kitchens and gave the servants their orders for feasts and banquets.

▶ Lord and lady of the manor.

8 The constable was in charge of defending the castle. He was usually a fierce and ruthless man. He trained his soldiers to guard the castle properly and organized the work schedule of guards and watchmen. The constable was in charge of the whole castle when the lord was away.

9 Many servants lived and worked inside the castle, looking after the lord and his family. They cooked, cleaned, served at table, worked as maids and servants, and ran errands. A man called the steward was in charge of all the servants.

Servants   Steward   Cooks

10

Inside the castle walls were many workshops where goods were made and repaired. The castle blacksmith was kept busy making shoes for all the horses. The armorer made weapons and armor.

Armorer

Blacksmith

▶ The master of the horse had to look after the lord's horses.

11

Local villagers would shelter in the castle when their lands were under attack. They were not allowed to shelter inside the keep itself, so they stayed inside the bailey with their families and all their animals.

From kings to peasants

12 In medieval times, the king or queen was the most important person in the country. The king gave land to his barons and other noblemen. In return, they supplied the king with soldiers, horses, and weapons to fight wars. This system of giving away land in return for services was known as feudalism.

▶ This bishop is having a meeting, called an audience, with the king and queen. In medieval times there was often conflict between the Church and the king. Both were very powerful, and they had to try to work together.

13 The Church was very powerful in the Middle Ages. It controlled large areas of land, and grew rich from the taxes paid by the peasants who worked on these lands. Peasant farmers had to give the church a tithe, one tenth of everything they produced.

14 The barons were the most powerful noblemen. A wealthy baron might supply the king with around 5,000 fighting men. Some barons also had their own private army to keep control over their own lands.

15 The wealthier lords and barons often gave away some of their lands to professional fighters called knights. Knights were skilled soldiers who rode into battle on horseback.

Quiz

1. What is the name of the mound of soil on which early castles were built?
2. Which was the safest and best-protected part of the castle?
3. What is a moat?
4. Who was in charge of the castle guards?
5. What did the king give to his lords in return for their services?

1. a motte 2. the keep 3. a water-filled ditch around the outside of the castle walls 4. the constable 5. land

16 At the very bottom of the feudal system was the poor peasant. In the Middle Ages over 90 percent of people living in Europe worked on the land. Everything in their lives—their land, animals, food, even their clothes—belonged to the local lord.

How to be a good knight

17 It took about 14 years of training to become a knight. The son of a noble joined a lord's household at age seven. He learned how to ride, to shoot a bow and arrow, and how to behave in front of nobles. He then became a squire, where he learned how to fight with a sword, and he looked after his master's armor and weapons. If he was successful, he became a knight at 21.

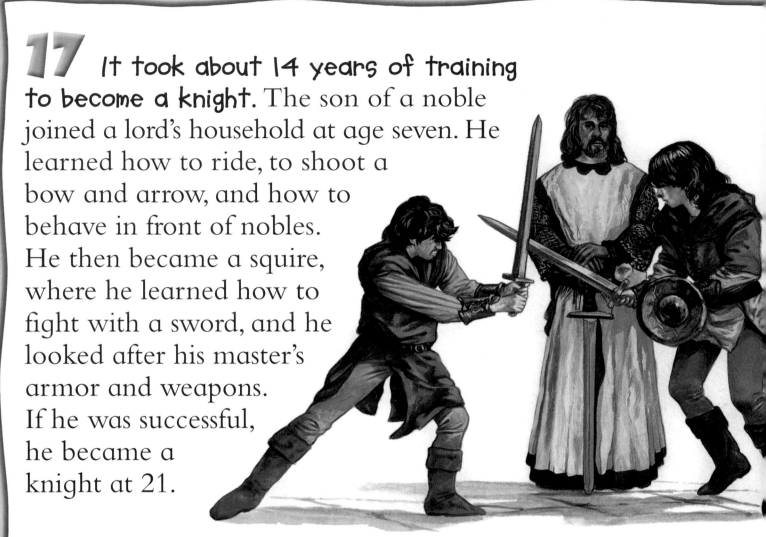

18 The ceremony of making a new knight was known as dubbing. A knight had to spend a whole night in church before his dubbing ceremony took place. This all-night watch was called a vigil. First, he had a cold bath and dressed in a plain white tunic. Then he spent the night on his knees in church, praying and confessing his sins.

19

The dubbing ceremony changed over time. In the beginning a knight was struck on the back of the neck. Later, dubbing involved a tap on the knight's shoulder with a sword.

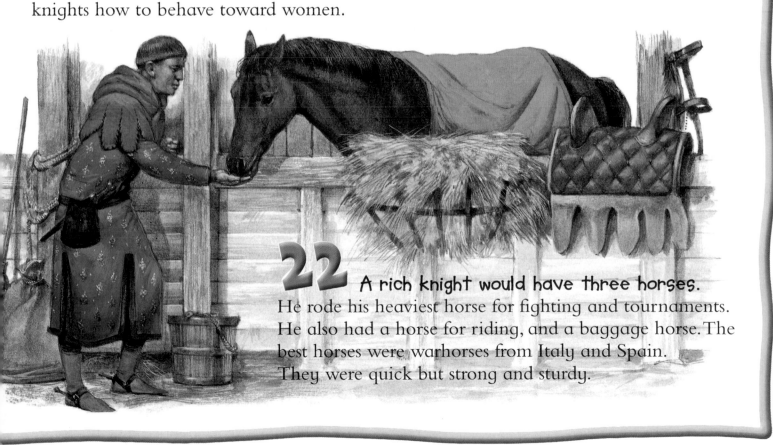

I DON'T BELIEVE IT!

A French knight named Jaufré Rudel sent love poems to the Countess of Tripoli even though he had never met her. When he finally saw her beautiful face he fell into her arms and died.

20

Knights had to behave according to a set of rules, known as the "code of chivalry." The code involved being brave and honorable on the battlefield, and treating the enemy politely and fairly. It also instructed knights how to behave toward women.

21

A knight who behaved badly was disgraced and punished. A knight in disgrace had either behaved in a cowardly way on the battlefield, cheated in a tournament, or treated another knight badly.

22

A rich knight would have three horses. He rode his heaviest horse for fighting and tournaments. He also had a horse for riding, and a baggage horse. The best horses were warhorses from Italy and Spain. They were quick but strong and sturdy.

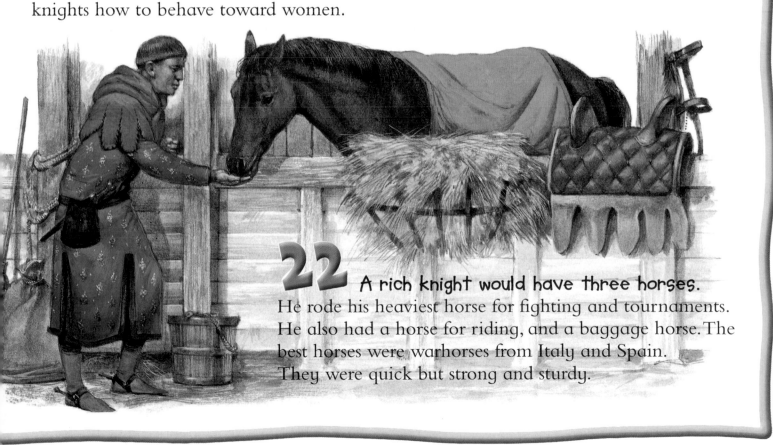

Ready for battle

23 Knights wore a long–sleeved tunic made of linen or wool, with a cloak over the top. By the 1200s knights had started to wear long hooded coats called surcoats. Knights nearly always wore bright colors, and some even wore fancy items such as shoes with curled pointed toes, and hats decorated with sparkling jewels.

◄ A knight was dressed for battle from the feet upward. The last item of armor to be put on him was his helmet.

25 Gradually, knights began to wear more and more armor. They added solid metal plates shaped to fit their body. By the 1400s knights were wearing full suits of steel armor. They wore metal gloves, called gauntlets, and even metal shoes!

26 A knight had two main weapons: his sword and his shield. The sword was double edged and was sharp enough to pierce chainmail. Knights also fought with lances, daggers, and axes.

24 Early knights wore a type of armor called chainmail. It was made of thousands of tiny iron rings joined onto each other. A piece of chainmail looked a bit like knitting, except it was made of metal, not wool. But a knight also wore a padded jacket under his chainmail to make sure he wasn't cut by his own armor!

◄ These knights are fighting in battle. The knight on the right has the usual weapons of a sword and shield. The knight on the left has a morning star. This was a spiked ball on the end of a chain.

27 Between 1337 and 1453 England and France were almost continually at war with each other, what we now know as the Hundred Years' War. The English armies won important battles against the French in 1356 and at Agincourt in 1415. The skilled English and Welsh longbowmen, who could fire as many as 12 arrows every minute, helped to stop the French knights.

28 A Swiss foot soldier's main weapon was a halberd. This was a combined spear and battle-ax, and was a particularly nasty, but very effective, way of a foot soldier getting a knight off his horse.

I DON'T BELIEVE IT!

Soldiers called "retrievers" used to have to run into the middle of the battle and collect up all the spare arrows!

Colors and coats of arms

29 When a knight went into battle in full armor wearing a helmet with a visor, no one could recognize him. This problem was solved by putting a different set of colored symbols on each knight's shield. These sets of symbols became known as coats of arms, and each family had its own personal design. No other family was allowed to use that design.

Heraldry, the system of using coats of arms, became a very complex system of signs and symbols. Schools of heraldry were set up to sort out disputes over coats of arms.

30 Only certain colors and styles of design could be used to create a coat of arms. The colors allowed were red, blue, black, green, purple, silver, and gold. The arms also indicated the wearer's position in his family. So, a second son showed a crescent symbol, and a seventh son displayed a rose.

31 On the battlefield, each nobleman had his own banner around which his knights and other soldiers could meet. The nobleman's colors and coat of arms were displayed on the banner. Banners decorated with coats of arms also made a colorful display at tournaments and parades.

◀ The banner of a nobleman was a very important symbol during battle. If the person holding the banner was killed in battle, someone had to pick the banner up and raise it straight away.

32 Messengers called heralds carried messages between knights during battle. They had to be able to recognize each individual knight quickly. After coats of arms were introduced, the heralds became experts at identifying them. The system of using coats of arms became known as heraldry.

▲ After a battle, it was the sad job of a herald to walk around the battlefield and identify the dead by their coats of arms.

DESIGN YOUR OWN COAT OF ARMS

Would you like your own personal coat of arms? You can design one by following the basic rules of heraldry explained on these pages. You will need the seven paint colors listed opposite, a paintbrush, a fine-tipped black felt pen, a ruler, and some thick white paper. Good luck!

Famous knights

33 Roland was a brave, loyal knight who died in the service of his master. Roland served King Charles the Great —Charlemagne—who ruled much of France and Germany in the 800s. Roland had to protect Charlemagne and his army from Muslim attackers as they crossed from Spain into France. But Roland was betrayed and died fighting for his king.

▲ Famous stories of old knights have been recorded in old books, like this one bound in leather.

34 The Spanish knight Rodrigo Díaz de Vivar had the nickname "El Cid." This comes from the Arabic for "the Lord." El Cid fought against the Moors from North Africa. He was exiled by his lord, King Alfonso VI, after the knight's enemies turned the king against him.

▼ Don Quixote charged at windmills because he thought they were giants.

▲ Rodrigo Díaz de Vivar, "El Cid."

35 The book "Don Quixote" tells the story of an old man who dreams about past deeds of bravery and chivalry. It was written in the 1500s by a Spaniard called Miguel de Cervantes. After reading about the knights of old, Don Quixote dresses in armor and sets off on horseback to become famous. He takes a peasant called Sancho Panzo with him as his squire, and it is his squire who gets Don Quixote out of trouble during his travels.

36 **Lancelot was the favorite knight of King Arthur.** Tales of Arthur and his Knights of the Round Table were very popular in the 1200s. Lancelot fell in love with Arthur's wife Guinevere. The struggle between the two men, and the scandal caused by the romance between Lancelot and Guinevere, eventually destroyed Arthur's court.

37 **The Black Prince was the nickname of Edward, the oldest son of Edward III of England.** The Black Prince was a great warrior who captured the French king, John II, at the battle of Poitiers in 1356.

I DON'T BELIEVE IT!

During his travels Don Quixote mistakes flocks of farmyard animals for enemy armies!

A castle tour

38 Stone castles were cold damp places with lots of drafts. A castle was not exactly a luxury home. Cold winds blew through the windows, which had no glass.

▶ The lord of the castle and his family were the only people who slept in beds. Most people slept on wooden pallets covered with straw.

▶ Almost all castles also had a well within their walls. This was essential as a source of water if someone laid siege to the castle.

▶ The kitchens were often built in a separate part of the castle, away from the keep, in case they caught fire.

Quiz

1. Which were the two main battle weapons of a knight?

2. Why did knights start to display a coat of arms?

3. Who was Sir Lancelot?

4. Who was the Black Prince?

5. What was the name of the castle toilet?

Answers:
1. a sword and a shield 2. to be recognized on the battlefield 3. the favorite knight of King Arthur 4. Prince Edward, the son of Edward III 5. the garderobe

▼ Castles had no central heating and no running water. Wool hangings and tapestries on the walls, and rugs on the floor, helped to warm the rooms. Roaring fires burned in the huge fireplaces.

39 There were many workshops and other buildings inside the safety of the castle walls. They included an armory, a smithy, stables, kennels, a mill for making flour, and a chapel. There were sometimes even gardens and orchards!

40 Medieval castles had no toilets! Instead people sat on wooden seats called "garderobes." These were built over a very long chute. Waste from the toilet fell down the chute into the moat.

◄ Every castle had a cold, dark, and often slimy dungeon for keeping prisoners. The dungeon was usually located beneath one of the gatehouse towers. Prisoners would be locked inside a small airless cell.

Feasts and fun

41 **The Great Hall was the centre of castle life.** The lord and his family ate their meals here and carried out their daily business. Colorful banners and coats of arms and shiny pieces of armor hung from the walls of the Great Hall. The hall was sometimes turned into a courtroom to try local law-breakers.

42 **Musicians entertained the lord and his guests at banquets in the Great Hall.** They played instruments such as pipes, drums, fiddles, and lutes.

43 **Jesters, jugglers, and acrobats performed for the diners between courses.** Sometimes a dancing bear might be brought in to entertain the guests.

BAKE A "TARTE OF APPLES AND ORANGES"

You will need:
a packet of shortcrust pastry
4 eating apples
4 oranges
juice of 1/2 lemon
3 cups of water
1 cup of honey
1/2 cup of brown sugar
1/4 tsp cinnamon
a pinch of dried ginger
a little milk
a little fine sugar

Ask an adult to help you. Line a pie dish with pastry and bake for 10 minutes in a medium-hot oven. Slice the oranges thinly. Boil the water, honey, and lemon juice, add the oranges. Cover and simmer for 2 hours, then drain. Peel, core, and slice the apples and mix with the sugar, cinnamon, and ginger. Place a layer of apples in the bottom of the dish followed by a layer of oranges, then alternate layers until the fruit is used up. Place a pastry lid over the top and brush with a little milk. Make small slits in the lid. Bake in a medium-hot oven for about 45 minutes.

44 Huge amounts of exotic-looking and delicious foods were served at banquets. Roast meats included stuffed peacock and swan, as well as venison, beef, goose, duck, and wild boar. Whole roasted fish were also served. These foods were followed by dishes made from spices brought from Asia, and then fruit and nuts.

45 The lord, his family, and important guests sat at the high table on a platform called a dais. From their raised position they could look down over the rest of the diners. The most important guests such as priests and noblemen sat next to the lord.

46 Important guests drank fine wine out of real glasses. Cup bearers poured the wine out of decorated pottery jugs. Less important diners drank ale or wine from mugs or tankards made of wood, pewter, or leather.

Songs, poems, and love

47 Medieval minstrels sang songs and recited poetry about love and bravery. These songs and poems showed knights as faithful, loving, and religious men who were prepared to die for their king or lard. A true knight fought for justice and fairness for everyone. In real life, knights did not always live up to this ideal picture.

◀ Minstrels sang their songs to the accompaniment of sweet-sounding music from a harp or lute.

▼ Knights offered to perform brave and heroic acts at tournaments to prove the strength of their love.

48 A style of romantic behavior called courtly love was popular among knights in both France and England. It was a kind of false love carried out by following strict rules. Courtly love stated that a knight had to fall in love with a woman of equal or higher rank—and ideally she should be married to someone else. Their love had to be kept secret.

49

Troubadours were poet-musicians who composed songs about heroic knights and ideal love. They lived in France in the 1100s and 1200s. Some troubadours had themselves been knights at one time, and they told rather exaggerated stories of their own deeds of love and bravery.

▲ Richard I of England, who is better known as Richard the Lionhearted, was a troubadour. Some of the songs he wrote have been preserved.

50

A knight wrote secret letters to the woman he loved. He had to worship his loved one from a distance, and could never declare his love for a lady directly to her.

▶ A knight and his love wrote poems to each other, expressing their feelings of love and devotion.

ILLUMINATED LETTERS

The first letter of a manuscript, called an illuminated letter, was much larger than the others, and it was decorated with pictures and patterns.

You can create your own set of illuminated letters for the initials of your name. Draw the outline of the letter in fine black pen and then use felt-tipped pens or paints to add the decoration.

▶ An illuminated letter "C."

Knights and dragons

51 The legend of St. George tells how the brave knight killed a fierce white dragon. The dragon was terrorizing the people of Lydia (part of modern Turkey). The king offered his daughter to the dragon if the dragon left his people alone. St. George arrived and said he would kill their dragon if they became Christians like him. Thousands accepted his offer, and George killed the dragon.

▲ St. George was adopted as the patron saint of England in the 1300s.

52 Ivanhoe was a medieval knight who lived in the time of Richard the Lionhearted. He is the hero of a historical book called "Ivanhoe," written by the Scottish novelist Sir Walter Scott in the 1800s. "Ivanhoe" describes the conflict between the Saxon people and their Norman conquerors at a time when the Normans had ruled England for at least 100 years.

53 Legend says that King Arthur became king after pulling a magic sword called Excalibur out of a stone. This act proved that he was the right person to rule Britain. People have written stories about Arthur and his followers, the Knights of the Round Table, for more than 1,000 years.

◄ No one really knows who the real Arthur was, but he may have been a Celtic warrior who lived about 1,400 years ago.

55 In the 1300s an Englishman called Geoffrey Chaucer wrote "The Canterbury Tales." These stories were about a group of pilgrims travelling from a London inn to a religious site in Canterbury. The pilgrims included a priest, a nun, a merchant, a cook, a plowman and a knight and his squire.

54 King Arthur had many castle homes but his favorite was Camelot. Historians think that Camelot was really an English castle called Tintagel. When Arthur heard that his best friend and favorite knight, Sir Lancelot, had fallen in love with Arthur's wife, Queen Guinevere, Arthur banished Lancelot from his court at Camelot.

Quiz

1. What is a minstrel?
2. Whose job was it to fill everyone's glass at a banquet?
3. What did a troubadour do?
4. Who were the Knights of the Round Table?
5. What is the name of King Arthur's favorite castle?

1. a wandering musician 2. the cup bearer 3. write songs about knights and courtly love 4. the followers of King Arthur 5. Camelot

Practice for battle

56 In a tournament, knights divided into two sides and fought each other as if in a real battle. Tournaments were good practice for the real thing—war. The idea for these mock battles, called tourneys, probably started in France in the 12th century.

▲ Edward I of England was a keen supporter of tournaments and jousts. He banned spectators from carrying weapons themselves because this caused too much trouble among the watching crowds.

▼ Jousting knights charged at each other at top speed. Each one tried to knock his opponent off his horse with a blow from a long wooden lance.

57
Tournaments took place under strict rules. There were safe areas where knights could rest without being attacked by the other side. Knights were not meant to kill their opponents but they often did. Several kings became so angry at losing their best knights that all tournaments were banned unless the king had given his permission.

58
Jousting was introduced because so many knights were being killed or wounded during tournaments. More than 60 knights were killed in a single tourney in Cologne, Germany. Jousting was a fight between two knights on horseback. Each knight tried to win by knocking the other off his horse. Knights were protected by armor, and their lances were not sharp.

59
A knight's code of chivalry did not allow him to win a tournament by cheating. It was better to lose with honor than to win in disgrace.

I DON'T BELIEVE IT!

Some knights cheated in jousts by wearing special armor that was fixed onto the horse's saddle!

60
Sometimes the knights carried on fighting on the ground with their swords. The problem was that this was as dangerous as a tourney!

61
A joust gave a knight the chance to prove himself in front of the woman he loved. Jousts were very social events watched by ladies of the court as well as ordinary people. Knights could show off their skills and bravery to impress the spectators.

Friend or enemy?

62 When Edward the Confessor died in 1066, Duke William of Normandy, his cousin, claimed that he had been promised the throne of England. William and his knights invaded England and defeated Harold, the English king, at the Battle of Hastings.

▲ The Bayeux Tapestry records the story of the Norman invasion of England. It shows William and his knights landing along the English coast, and also shows the moment when England's King Harold was killed at the Battle of Hastings.

▲ Here you can see the route that William the Conqueror took to London.

63 On and off between 1337 and 1453 the neighboring countries of England and France were at war. The Hundred Years' War, as it was called, carried on through the reigns of five English kings and five French ones. The two countries fought each other to decide who should control France. In the end the French were victorious, and England lost control of all her lands in France apart from the port of Calais.

64 One of the major battles of the Hundred Years' War was fought at Crécy in 1346. English soldiers defeated a much larger French army, killing almost half the French soldiers. During the battle, the English army used gunpowder and cannons for possibly the first time.

65

Deadly weapons called caltrops were used in the Hundred Years' War. A caltrop was a star-shaped piece of metal. These were scattered along the ground in front of an attacking army. They stopped both horses and footsoldiers in their tracks.

66

A young French girl known as Joan of Arc led the French army against the English, who had surrounded the city of Orléans. After 10 days the English were defeated. Joan was later captured, accused of being a witch, and burned to death.

I DON'T BELIEVE IT!

If you captured a knight alive during battle, you could offer him back to his family in return for a generous ransom!

Under attack

67 An attacking enemy had to break through a castle's defenses to get inside its walls. One method was to break down the castle gates with giant battering rams. Attackers and defenders also used siege engines to hurl boulders at each other.

68 A siege is when an enemy surrounds a castle and stops all supplies from reaching the people inside. The idea is to starve the castle occupants until they surrender or die.

69 A riskier way of trying to get inside a castle was to climb over the walls. Attackers either used ladders or moved wooden towers with men hidden inside them into position beside the walls.

70

Giant catapults were sometimes uses to fire stones or burning pieces of wood inside the castle. The Romans were some of the first people to use catapults in warfare.

► Attackers could also dig a tunnel under a wall or a tower. They would then light a fire that burned away the tunnel's supports. The tunnel collapsed, and brought down the building above.

▲ This siege engine was called a trebuchet. It had a long wooden arm with a heavy weight at one end and a sling at the other. A heavy stone was placed inside the sling. As the weight dropped, the stone was hurled toward the castle walls, sometimes traveling as far as 1,000ft (300m).

71

The enemy sometimes succeeded in tunneling beneath the castle walls. They surprised the defenders when they appeared inside the castle itself.

I DON'T BELIEVE IT!

The ropes used to wind up siege catapults were made from plaits of human hair!

► Cannons were first used to attack castles and fortified towns and cities in the 1300s. Early cannons, called bombards, were made of bronze or iron and they were not very accurate.

72

The invention of cannons and gunpowder brought the building of castle strongholds almost to an end. It marked the end of warrior knights too. Castle walls could not stand up to the powerful cannonballs that exploded against them. Guns and cannons were now used on the battlefield, so armies no longer needed the services of brave armored knights on horseback.

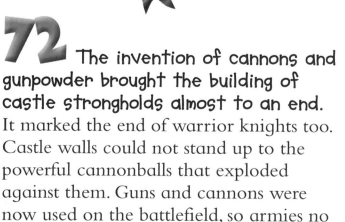

Defending a castle

73 When the enemy was first spotted approaching a castle, its defenders first pulled up the castle **drawbridge.** They also lowered an iron grate, called a portcullis, to form an extra barrier behind the drawbridge.

74 The castle archers fired their arrows through narrow slits in the thick castle **walls.** They also fired through the gaps in the battlements.

◄ Crossbows were far slower to aim and fire than longbows.

▶ Soldiers could use a longbow while the enemy was still a long way away.

75 In the middle of the night, a raiding party might leave a besieged castle to surprise the enemy camped outside. The raiders would move along secret passages and climb out through hidden gates or doorways.

76 Defenders poured boiling-hot water onto the heads of the enemy as they tried to climb the castle walls. Quicklime was also poured over the enemy soldiers, making their skin burn.

▶ Water was poured onto the enemy's heads through holes in the stonework of the battlements.

77 Heavy stones and other missiles often rained down from the battlements onto the enemy below. Hidden from view by the high battlements, the defenders stood on wooden platforms to throw the missiles.

Quiz

1. What is the name of the mock battles held between large numbers of knights?

2. Which weapon did jousting knights use when on horseback?

3. Which two countries fought a war that lasted 100 years?

4. In what year was the battle of Agincourt?

5. Which machine was used to break down castle walls and gates?

1. tourneys 2. a lance 3. England and France 4. 1415 5. a battering ram

Off to the crusades

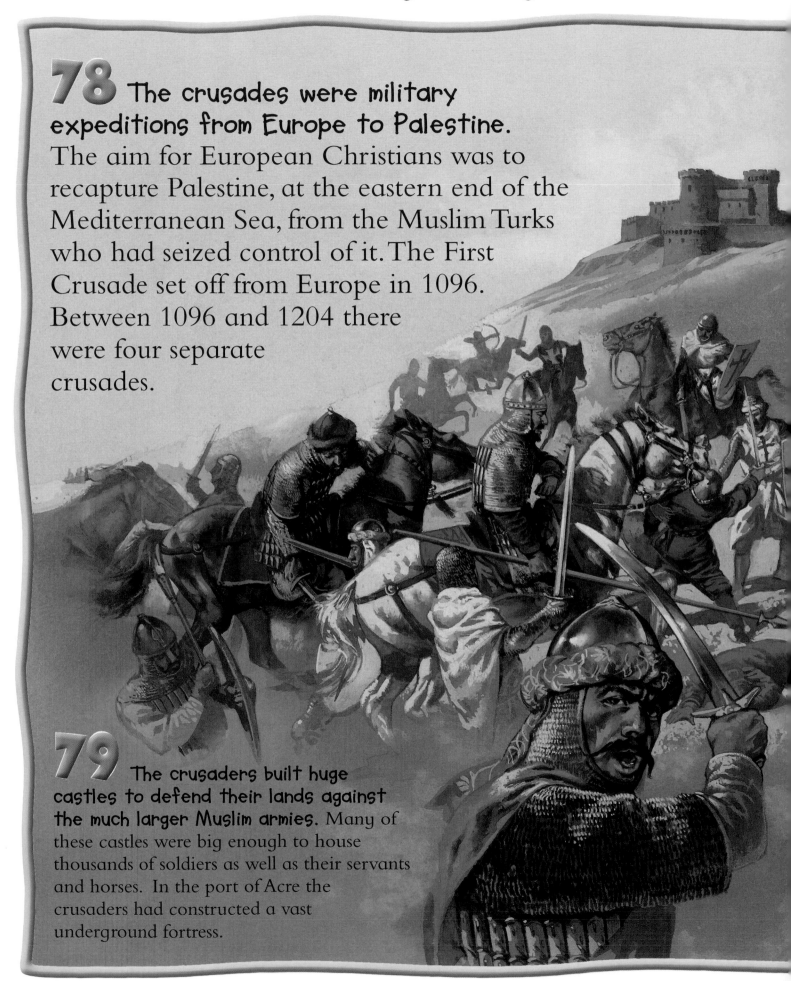

78 The crusades were military expeditions from Europe to Palestine. The aim for European Christians was to recapture Palestine, at the eastern end of the Mediterranean Sea, from the Muslim Turks who had seized control of it. The First Crusade set off from Europe in 1096. Between 1096 and 1204 there were four separate crusades.

79 The crusaders built huge castles to defend their lands against the much larger Muslim armies. Many of these castles were big enough to house thousands of soldiers as well as their servants and horses. In the port of Acre the crusaders had constructed a vast underground fortress.

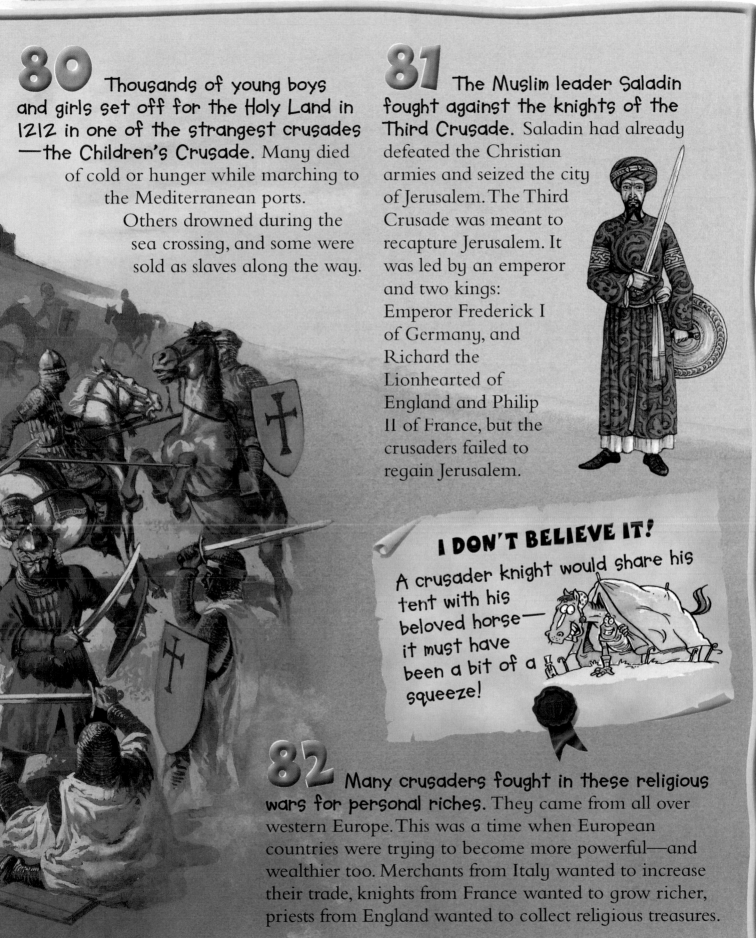

80

Thousands of young boys and girls set off for the Holy Land in 1212 in one of the strangest crusades—the Children's Crusade. Many died of cold or hunger while marching to the Mediterranean ports. Others drowned during the sea crossing, and some were sold as slaves along the way.

81

The Muslim leader Saladin fought against the knights of the Third Crusade. Saladin had already defeated the Christian armies and seized the city of Jerusalem. The Third Crusade was meant to recapture Jerusalem. It was led by an emperor and two kings: Emperor Frederick I of Germany, and Richard the Lionhearted of England and Philip II of France, but the crusaders failed to regain Jerusalem.

I DON'T BELIEVE IT!

A crusader knight would share his tent with his beloved horse—it must have been a bit of a squeeze!

82

Many crusaders fought in these religious wars for personal riches. They came from all over western Europe. This was a time when European countries were trying to become more powerful—and wealthier too. Merchants from Italy wanted to increase their trade, knights from France wanted to grow richer, priests from England wanted to collect religious treasures.

Garters and elephants

83 A group of Christian knights living in the Holy Land were in charge of protecting pilgrims on their way to and from Palestine. They were the Templar knights, or Templars. Their headquarters were in the Aqsa Mosque in the city of Jerusalem. The Templars grew very rich during their time in the Holy Land, but their organization was eventually broken up.

84 The Knights of St. John looked after the safety and health of pilgrims while they were in the Holy Land. The knights lived like monks and followed strict rules, but they also continued to provide soldiers to fight the Muslims.

▶ The Knights of St. John had been monks who cared for sick people before becoming religious knights. They were often referred to as the Hospitalers.

85 Medieval knights began to band together to form special groups called orders. Each order had its own badge showing the symbol chosen by the order. It was considered an honor to be asked to join an order. New orders began to appear in many countries across Europe. The Order of the Golden Fleece, for example, was started in France by Philip the Good.

▲ Knights wore the badge of their order on a chain around the neck. Knights from the Order of the Golden Fleece wore a badge depicting a golden sheep.

86

The Order of the Bath was founded in Britain in the early 1400s. Knights who belonged to an order swore loyalty to their king or queen, and promised to fight against their enemies.

87

The Order of the Garter is the oldest and most important order in Britain. According to the story, Edward III was dancing with a countess when she lost her garter. As the king gave it back to her, he heard the people near him laughing and joking about what they had seen. Angry, the king said that anyone who had evil thoughts should be ashamed. This is still the motto of the order.

▼ The emblem of the Order of the Garter is a dark–blue garter trimmed with gold. Knights of the order wear it on their left leg at important ceremonies.

Quiz

1. Which Muslim warrior fought against the knights of the Third Crusade?

2. By what other name is Richard I of England known?

3. In which city can you find important Muslim and Christian sites?

4. What do knights of the Order of the Golden Fleece wear around their necks?

1. Saladin
2. Richard the Lionhearted
3. Jerusalem
4. a golden sheep

88

The Order of the Elephant from Denmark is more than 500 years old. Members of the order wear a badge that features a elephant waving its trunk in the air.

Warriors from the East

89 Warrior knights in Japan in the Middle Ages were known as samurai. People in Japan were also divided into different feudal groups, where people in each group served someone in a higher-ranking group. The samurai, like European knights, served a lord. They usually fought on horseback but later on they began to fight more on foot.

▼ The Seljuk Turks were named after their first leader, Seljuk.

90 A long curving sword was a samurai warrior's most treasured possession. Samurai warriors wore armor on the bodies, arms, and legs, a helmet, and often a crest made up of a pair of horns.

91 The fierce Seljuk Turks fought against Christian knights during the crusades. The Seljuks swept across southwest Asia in the 1000s and 1100s. They conquered many lands, including Syria, Palestine, Asia Minor (modern Turkey), and Persia (modern Iran).

92 Fierce Mongol warriors from the East terrifed the enemy in battle. The Mongols were expert horsemen who controlled their horses with their feet while standing up in their stirrups. This way of riding left both hands free to shoot a bow and arrow.

▼ Each Mongol warrior had a team of five horses ready for battle. As well as being skilled archers, the Mongols were highly trained spear-throwers.

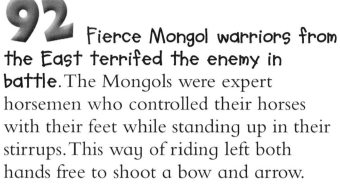

93 Genghis Khan was the greatest of the Mongol leaders. He became leader of his tribe when he was just 13 years old. He united all the Mongol tribes, and went on to conquer northern China, Korea, northern India, Afghanistan, Persia, and parts of Russia.

I DON'T BELIEVE IT!

The Turks fought with gold pieces in their mouth—to stop the crusader knights from stealing their gold. If a Turkish warrior thought he was going to die, he swallowed the gold.

Famous castles

94 Many castles are said to be haunted by the ghosts of people who died within their walls. Many of these ghosts are kings and queens who were killed by their sworn enemies. Edward II of England was murdered in his cell at Berkeley Castle in southwest England. Richard II died at Pontefract Castle in Yorkshire.

▲ Visitors to Berkeley Castle say they can hear the screams of the murdered Edward at night.

▲ Windsor Castle.

95 English kings and queens have lived at Windsor Castle since William the Conqueror began building it more than 900 years ago. William's original castle consisted of a wooden fort on top of an earth motte, with earthworks around the bailey area. The first stone buildings were added in the 1100s.

96 Glamis Castle in Scotland is the scene for the play "Macbeth" by William Shakespeare. In the play, the ambitious Macbeth plots with his evil wife to kill the Scottish king, Duncan, and claim the throne for himself. In real life, Macbeth did defeat and kill Duncan in 1040.

▼ Glamis Castle.

▲ Bodiam Castle.

97 The moated Bodiam Castle in southern England was built in the 1300s to keep out attacking French armies. An English knight, Sir Edward Dalyngrigge, believed that the French were about to invade his lands. His castle home had a curtain wall broken up by round towers.

▼ The castle at Krak des Chevaliers that visitors see today is almost unchanged from the 1300s and 1400s. This remarkable castle was the home of the Hospitaller knights.

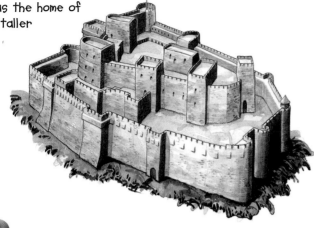

98 The huge crusader castle of Krak des Chevaliers in Syria is perched on a hill of solid rock with far-reaching views over the surrounding countryside. A ditch between the castle's massive outside wall, with its 13 towers, and the inside wall was filled with water from a nearby aqueduct. This moat was used to supply the castle baths and to water the knights' horses.

99 The town of Carcassonne in southern France is rather like one huge castle. The whole town is surrounded by high walls and towers that were built in the Middle Ages.

100 The hilltop castle of Neuschwanstein was built long after the Middle Ages—work on the castle started in 1869. The fairytale castle was the dream project of "mad" King Ludwig of Bavaria. The government of Bavaria removed the king from power because his ambitious castle-building plans cost too much money.

◀ Today, Neuschwanstein Castle is one of Germany's most popular tourist attractions. The castle was the model for the Magic Kingdom castle in Disneyland.

Index